Stories from yorkshire monasteries

Joan and Bill Spence

Illustrations by
Geraldine Jones, Dip AD, RAPGC, SGFA and

Judith Gilbert, Dip AD, ATD
Artist in Residence Bradford Cathedral

Foreword by
His Eminence Cardinal Dom Basil Hume,
O.S.B., M.A., S.T.L., D.D.(Hon)

Highgate Publications (Beverley) Limited, 1993

For Joan who enjoyed the monasteries with me

©ISBN 0 948929 66 9

Published by Highgate Publications (Beverley) Ltd.
24 Wylies Road, Beverley, HU17 7AP
Telephone (0482) 866826

Printed and Typeset in 10 on 11pt Plantin by
Colourspec, Unit 7, Tokenspire Park, Hull Road,
Woodmansey, Beverley, HU17 8EG
Telephone (0482) 864264

CIP Data Available

Also by Joan and Bill Spence
The Medieval Monasteries of Yorkshire
Romantic Ryedale
Handy Facts — North Yorkshire

CONTENTS

ARCHBISHOP'S HOUSE,

WESTMINSTER, LONDON, SWIP 1QJ

15 March, 1993

Monasticism flourished in Yorkshire in medieval times. Its influence spread far beyond this country and in many ways has persisted through the ages even to the present day. Ruined monasteries still bear witness to that great age.

Here in this book stories of fact and fiction, which have grown up around the lives of those early monks, are told by Joan and Bill Spence. They stem from their long-standing interest in monasticism. The stories were gathered as they researched their earlier book, "The Medieval Monasteries of Yorkshire". In telling them they bring life to the stones which stand silent witnesses to the great age of monasticism.

The delightful illustrations, pen and ink and scraperboard, by their twin daughters, Geraldine Jones and Judith Gilbert, are an added attraction to a book which brings entertaining reading to a subject too often regarded as dull.

I am happy to be associated with this book for Joan and Bill Spence, and their family, have been life-long personal friends.

Basil Hume

Archbishop of Westminster

CHAPTER ONE

BROTHER JUCUNDUS

Benedictine monks who had established a monastery at Lastingham, on the site of St. Cedd's monastery destroyed by the Danes, found the area remote and hostile and left it for York.

In 1088-89 St. Mary's Abbey was founded close to the River Ouse and near to St. Peter's Hospital which had been established in 936 by King Athelstan. It was renamed St. Leonard's in 1142 by King Stephen. It was the most important hospital of the 23 in medieval York. Apart from nursing the sick, these hospitals were homes for the aged and homeless. They were almshouses, and St. Leonard's had an orphanage and a small choir school. At its height of importance it was staffed by four secular priests, 13 brothers, eight sisters and six labourers, all under the rule of a Master.

But things did not always run smoothly. On one occasion after an examination the Master was told to govern with more consideration and to tighten discipline. The brothers could only leave the hospital for a good reason with the Master's permission, and, if that were given, they must be accompanied by another brother. They had to avoid drinking parties and were to eat and drink only at the set times. They were not allowed to partake of food or drink outside the hospital and were not to dine with the sisters.

The story goes that one of the brothers, Brother Jucundus, before joining the brethren, had led a jovial life and had enjoyed his food and especially his wine. Now he found, while desiring to pursue charitable works, that the stricter life was a tax. He longed for the old life, unfettered by strict rules and free of frugality.

One day, realising it was the day of the fair, he recalled the lively times he used to have and, within the confines of the hospital walls, imagined the gaiety which would be going on outside. It was too much for him and he decided he must taste the old life once more. If he could sneak out and back without any of his brethren seeing him no one need be any the wiser. But he would need some spending money. He awaited his opportunity and, when the Master was out of his room, he slipped in and took a crown from the alms-box. He was a step nearer the frivolity he longed for. Excitement did not dull his caution and, without being seen, he slipped out of the hospital and mingled with the crowds. He was swept into the merry-making and his

2

old jocular self soon emerged. He had a merry time visiting the sideshows, partaking of the sweetmeats he had missed so much and quaffing tankard after tankard of ale and wine. There was joy in his heart, laughter in his eyes and on his lips. But that joy froze with shock, the laughter died, his eyes dulled, his lips set in a grim line and his mind momentarily sobered as the vision of the austere life within the walls of St. Leonard's manifested itself at the sight of two of his brethren watching him with eyes wide with astonishment.

Once the initial shock had broken he tried to laugh the matter off by inviting his brothers to join in the frivolity. Alas for Brother Jucundus, they were of a much more determined nature and within a few minutes were escorting him back to St. Leonard's. There he faced the Master and his other brethren. The two brothers who had found him related what they had seen and Brother Jucundus pleaded his own case with regret and sorrow as well as he could in his inebriated state. But that was not enough. He had broken all the rules and must be punished as his crime merited. He was condemned to die a slow agonising death by being walled up.

He was led away, seated on a stool in a corner of the cellars, and given a jug of water and a loaf of bread. As sombre as the occasion was, as he watched his brethren slowly build a wall around him, he laughed and joked with them. Still under the influence of the drink he started to sing, and the brothers, their task done, could still hear him singing as they left the cellars.

Brother Jucundus fell asleep and it was not until he woke in a much more sober frame of mind that he realised that his fate was a slow death by starvation in complete darkness. In desperation he tried to free himself. He beat at the newly made walls, pushed and shoved them, but his brethren had done their work too well. He tried harder by levering himself with his back against the cellar wall. He felt this wall give. At first he thought it was his imagination but he pushed harder. Suddenly the wall gave way and he fell out of his place of incarceration amidst tumbling stones and mortar. For a few moments he lay, with dust settling around him, trying to make out where he was. This was not a familiar part of the hospital to him and in his hazy mind he remembered sitting on a stool against an outside wall of the cellar.

He scrambled to his feet, dusted himself down and set off to explore. He found some stairs leading upwards. Reaching the top he found a door unlocked, and gingerly opened it. Peering out he saw a corridor. No one was about so he slipped out and set off to discover where he was. Seeing some monks going about their business silently, he realised that at some part the cellars of St. Leonard's Hospital must have abutted the cellars of St. Mary's Abbey. He could continue his life here and no one would be any wiser, for the St. Mary's community was a large one and he could easily be taken for a new member.

So Brother Jucundus settled down to his new life only to find it was harder and more austere than that at St. Leonard's, but he had to put up with it and make of it what he could. After some time the Cellarer of St. Mary's died and the Abbot, having noted the conscientious piety of Brother Jucundus, made him the new Cellarer. If only he had known of the brother's liking for wine! The temptation was too great. Brother Jucundus had the key to great delights!

When it came to the meal at which the monks were allowed ale, Brother Jucundus, who should have brought it from the cellar, was not in the refectory. The monks waited. They became restless and the Abbot became more and more annoyed. Brother Jucundus must be found. The Abbot ordered a search which led him to the cellar. There they found a very happy brother who had partaken of the very best wine which was kept for very special guests. It was all gone, and more besides. Brother Jucundus greeted his fellow monks with a song and joviality which the Abbot determined should be dealt with there and then. Such a serious flagrancy of the laws of the community could not be left until later.

The punishment was swiftly decided by those in authority, and for the second time Brother Jucundus was walled up in a cellar, the wall being erected where the very stones had fallen on his first escape from a lingering death. In his happy frame of mind he was still singing when the final stone was placed in position and the monks of St. Mary's filed away, back to their austere life.

A short time later the Cellarer of St. Leonard's hospital came to draw the ale for the meal, a solemn one, for the Master had just died. The Cellarer froze to the spot when he entered the cellar. Singing! Coming from the very place where they had walled up Brother Jucundus a year ago.

It couldn't be. He inclined his head, listening intently. Yes it was — singing. His eyes widened with fright. A ghost! Brother Jucundus had come back to haunt them. The brother fled in terror, causing havoc among his brethren, sad and sorrowful at the death of their Master. They looked on the Cellarer with doubt and suspicion. What had he been up to? But he insisted that he had heard singing and persuaded the brothers to come and hear for themselves.

On reaching the cellar they too were amazed and frightened by what they heard. There was only one way to lay this ghost, release it from its prison and exorcize the spot. The brothers bent their backs with a will, only too eager to tear down the wall and get rid of the evil spirit. Then they fell back in amazement. Brother Jucundus! Alive after a year walled up. Alive and well, though maybe a little thinner than when they had last seen him.

This was a miracle, and, on this day when their Master had died, it could only mean one thing: Brother Jucundus was meant to be Master! He was installed into that office and ruled with less austerity until the day he died.

CHAPTER TWO

THE MYSTERY OF THE COFFIN LIDS

Tiny Hodge Beck escapes from Bransdale, a lonely dale cut into the North York Moors, passes through Sleightholmedale and flows into Kirkdale. The northern end of Kirkdale is gorge-like and a minor road, once the main road between the market towns of Helmsley and Kirbymoorside, plunges across Hodge Beck close to the oldest archaeological site in North Yorkshire.

Nearby is ancient St. Gregory's Minster standing amidst the seclusion of cypress trees. Sheltered by the porch is a Saxon sundial set in the wall above the simple Norman doorway. The sundial is carved on a stone seven feet long with an inscription in a perfect state of preservation. In the English of a few years before the Norman Conquest is written:

> 'Orm Gamal's Son bought St. Gregory's Minster when it was all broken down and fallen and he let it be made anew from the ground to Christ and St. Gregory, in Edward's days, the King, and in Tosti's days, the Earl.'

From this we know that the church was rebuilt when Edward the Confessor (1042-1066) was King, but the date narrows with the reference to Tosti who was Earl of Northumberland from 1055 to 1065.

The inscription also tells us that there was a church on the site before this, so the Saxon crosses and coffin lids inserted in the walls may well have been from this pre-Norman church. Early this century two interesting stone slabs were removed from the west wall and placed in the church, where they can be seen today. There is a theory that they may be the coffin lids, or grave slabs, of St. Cedd and King Ethelwald. One of these has a fine carving of a cross and it is said that there were also the words, in runic characters, *Cyning Aethilwald*, though these can no longer be deciphered.

It is known that Ethelwald, son of King Oswald, gave land to St. Cedd to build a monastery:

> 'Ethelwald, the son of King Oswald who reigned among the Deiri, finding him a holy, wise and good man, desired him to accept some land to build a monastery, to which he himself

6

might frequently resort to offer his prayers and hear the word, and be buried in it when he died.'

Bede refers to the site as *Lestingau* and this has always been taken to be Lastingham, a few miles away. But why should the tombs of founder and patron be at Kirkdale if this is the case?

Monks took precious relics with them when they fled from their monasteries during the Danish raids on the north of England and the Lastingham monks could easily have taken the remains of St. Cedd and King Ethelwald with them when their monastery was attacked. It is possible they sought refuge in the monastery in remote Kirkdale, but this monastery was also attacked by the marauders. Could it be that this assault was so sudden that the monks had no time to escape and that none survived to tell the story of how the bodies of St. Cedd and King Ethelwald had been brought there?

Another theory is that the monastery at Kirkdale was the original monastery founded by St. Cedd, but this is less likely. It may be that these are not the coffin lids of these two holy men. Nothing is certain. It all happened long ago and any written records the monks would certainly have kept were destroyed by the Danes.

"Caedmon, sing some song to me... ...sing about the Creation of all things."

CHAPTER THREE

ST. HILDA

Troops under Oswy, Christian King of Northumbria, faced the pagan troops commanded by the fiercesome Penda at Winwaed, near Leeds, in 655.

Penda was determined to re-establish paganism throughout the north, something he had done twice before by defeating in battle Edwin, in 633, and Oswald, in 642, Oswy knew he was facing a formidable foe but, determined to be rid of the pagan threat once and for all, he dedicated himself and his army to God, sure that with God's help he would be victorious. As he prayed for victory he made a vow that if he triumphed he would dedicate his daughter, Aelfleda, to God and denote land throughout his kingdom on which to build twelve monasteries. After a fierce battle, in which at times it looked as though Penda would win, the forces of Christianity prevailed, Oswy was triumphant and paganism was banished forever.

At the time of this important victory, Hilda was abbess of a monastery at Hartlepool on the north bank of the River Tees. She was related to the royal house of Northumbria and had been baptised into the Christian faith at York, along with her great uncle, Edwin, by Paulinus in 627 when she was 13. Although she enjoyed life she felt drawn to serve God and when she was 30 she decided to enter the religious life of the community at Chelles, near Paris, where her sister was already living. However, Aidan, Bishop of Lindisfarne, whom she knew very well, persuaded her to remain in this country. He granted her land on the north bank of the River Wear at Monkwearmouth, where she and some companions could live a secluded life devoted to God.

A year later, when the Abbess of Hartlepool left to found a monastery near Tadcaster, Hilda was persuaded to take over the abbacy of the first convent for nuns in England. King Oswy knew of her devotion and ability as the head of a religious house. To fulfil his vow, after defeating Penda, he granted land at Whitby, *Streoneshalh*, 'the bay of the lighthouse', as it was known then, and asked her to establish a monastery there and to take into her care his daughter Aelfleda and bring her up in the religious life.

The monastery which Hilda founded, high on the windswept cliffs overlooking the North Sea, did not belong to any particular order. It was a double foundation where a community of nuns and a community of monks, devout Christians, shared a common ideal and, by free consent, placed themselves under the rule of a superior whom they respected, and in whom they saw great religious devotion, wisdom and quality of leadership.

Hilda was such a person and she ruled with such tact, diplomacy, and wisdom that her abbey became the scholastic as well as the religious focal point in the country.

St. Bede wrote of her:

> 'So great was her wisdom that not only ordinary folk but kings and princes used to come and ask her advice in their difficulties. All her acquaintances called her Mother because of her wonderful devotion and grace.'

The 12th-century historian, William of Malmesbury, reports that the abbey at Streoneshalh was the largest of the abbeys founded by King Oswy. Its influence was widespread, for from among its inmates came: Bosa, Bishop of York 678-705; St. John of Beverley, Bishop of Hexham 687, Bishop of York, 705-718: Wilfid II Bishop of York, 718-732; Hedda, Bishop of Dorchester; Ostfor, first Bishop of Worcester, 691-692.

Such was the reputation of Hilda's abbey that it was chosen as the place to hold a synod in 664.

The Church in Britain which had survived the pagan hordes was strong in the traditions and followings of the Celtic monks from Ireland and Scotland. After St. Augustine and his Benedictine missionaries, who followed the Continental religious observances, had brought Christianity to the south of Britain through Kent, it was inevitable that the two streams of Christian tradition should clash. The Synod of Whitby was convened to try to reconcile these differences, the main being the date on which Easter, the most important feast in the Church, should be kept. In 325, the Council of Nice had ruled that Easter Sunday should be the first Sunday after the first full moon after the Spring equinox. The Roman Church dated the equinox as 21 March but the Celtic Church placed it on 25 March. The difference in these dates could affect the date of Easter by as much as a month and so, if both traditions prevailed, part of the kingdom could be celebrating Easter while the rest of the people were still following the Lenten observances in preparation for Easter. There were strong divisions at the Synod with eminent churchmen and women supporting each case. However, the outcome was that the Celtic Church gave way so that one Christian viewpoint on this important matter and on several other minor ones could be held throughout the country.

That Whitby was chosen for such an important synod, at which so many Church dignitaries were present, shows the high esteem in which Hilda was held by the Church. Naturally, stories have grown around such a remarkable woman. One concerns her arrival at Streoneshalh. She found all around the site designated for her monastery, and in the valley of the Esk and its adjacent moors, deadly serpents.

> 'They lurked in the shrogs and bushes about it [the monastery],
> to the great terror of her and her nuns.'

She prayed for help to drive them into the sea. After praying she was directed to take a whip and confront the serpents. Wielding her whip she drove them to the edge of the cliffs and beheaded them before they fell over the edge. As they tumbled to the rocks and sea far below, their writhing bodies curled up and, when they reached the bottom, they were turned to stone.

> '...called to this day, by the country people, from this supposed
> miracle, St. Hilda's Stones, having the appearance of serpents
> or snakes rolled up or in their coil.'

Geologists recognise them as amonites or fossilised sea creatures, turned to stone by the pressure of rocks through the ages.

Another legend tells us that in mid-morning, during the summer, when the sun's rays fall on the north side of the choir, St. Hilda appears, in her glorified state, in one of the highest windows.

Local people believed that when sea birds and those on their migration flights rested on the cliffs they were paying homage to St. Hilda, and that the abbey was so holy that wild geese would never fly over it.

For the last seven years of her life Hilda was in ill-health, but she continued to rule and direct her community with wisdom and understanding including a subsidiary foundation of Hackness, 13 miles south of Whitby.

Hilda died in 680.

At Hackness, Bega, who had led a devout life for 30 years was asleep in the dormitory when she heard the tolling of a bell which, at that time of night, could only mean one thing: that one of their community had passed away. As she opened her eyes she saw a great light, in the midst of which Hilda was being taken to heaven by angels. Looking around the dormitory she saw her companions were fast asleep, and realised that in her sleep she had heard the bell of Streoneshalh, for Hackness had not one of its own. She hastened to her immediate superior, Frigyth, Abbess of Hackness. On hearing her story, Frigyth aroused all the other members of the small community and called them to pray for Hilda.

When news of Hilda's death arrived from Streoneshalh the time of death coincided exactly with the time when Bega had had her vision. One of the nuns of Streoneshalh also had a similar vision: being in a remote part of the monastery, in charge of newcomers to the order, she could not have known that Hilda had died, and yet her vision had occurred at the very moment of death.

Perhaps the best known story of Hilda is her connection and influence on Caedmon and the birth of English Literature. Among the manual labourers who worked for the monastery was a quiet, uneducated herdsman who kept very much to himself. Caedmon took no part in the singing and story telling which took place among the servants after the evening meal.

One evening he left the gathering for the cliff top. As he lay in the grass, watching the myriad of stars, the shining figure of an angel appeared to him. Startled by the sudden intrusion, Caedmon was gripped by fear until the angel spoke in a gentle, reassuring voice: 'Caedmon, the Lord wants you to sing for Him.' Caedmon was surprised at the use of his name, but felt sure that the angel had come to the wrong person: 'Alas I cannot. I don't know how. My voice is useless and I know no words. That is why I come out here, so that my fellows cannot mock my ignorance.'

'But the Lord wants thee to,' insisted the angel.

'But...' quaking, Caedmon started to protest.

'Thou can. Sing of the beginning of created things,' insisted the angel.

Caedmon hesitated and then suddenly found himself singing. The words, following the angel's suggested subject, came in the form of a poem.

After Caedmon had finished his song the angel bade him farewell and vanished. Caedmon, shaken by the experience, stared around him hoping to find some explanation of the experience, but all he saw was the vastness of the night sky pricked by the beauty of the stars, and all he heard was the gentle lap of the waves on the foot of the cliffs far below. In this serenity, puzzling over what had happened, Caedmon fell asleep.

The next morning when he awoke he recalled the incident vividly in every detail. At first he was inclined to keep it to himself, but then he felt compelled to tell someone. He went to his superior who, on hearing the tale, decided it was a matter for the Abbess. He took Caedmon to Hilda, who recognised the work of God in the incident. She took Caedmon into the monastery so that he could set down in song and verse the first poem in the English tongue:

'Now must we praise the Warden of Heaven's realm,
The Creator's might and his mind's thought,
The glorious works of the Father: how of every wonder
He, the Lord Eternal, laid the foundation.
He shaped erst, for the sons of men,
Heaven as their roof, Holy Creator.
The middle world, He, mankind's Warden,
Eternal Lord, afterwards prepared,
The Earth for men, Lord Almighty.'

When St. Hilda died she was succeeded as Abbess by Aelfleda, King Oswy's daughter, whom he had pledged to the Church. She reigned until 713, and there is no record of any nun succeeding her. It seems likely that a monk was elected to the position of Abbot, superior to the whole establishment.

This widely known and influential monastery lay in the path of the marauding Danes and was destroyed by them in 867.

CHAPTER FOUR

THE HOLY BROTHERS

In the tiny village of Lastingham, nestling in the southern folds of the North York Moors, there in one of the most complete Norman crypts in the country. Apart from being a complete church in itself, having a chancel, nave and aisles, the crypt is unique in being one of the few in the country to have an apse. The short pillars with heavy bases and capitals support simple round arches. The nave has a groined rubble vaulting while the chancel has a simple barrel vault.

It was built by Stephen and his monks between 1078 and 1086. They had left their monastery at Whitby to found another, and chose Lastingham, no doubt because of its holy connections, four centuries earlier. Cedd, a member of the monastery on Lindisfarne, off the Northumbrian coast, was sent, with three others, in 653, to help in evangelising the Kingdom of Mercia, and then with an assistant to convert the East Saxons. Though diligent and thorough in his work he always yearned to be back in his beloved Northumbria, the kingdom which stretched from the Humber northwards. Whilst carrying out this work he was recalled to Lindisfarne and created a bishop.

Ethelwald, King of Deira, an area corresponding roughly with what we know as Yorkshire, wished to meet Cedd, and this was arranged through Coelin, who was the King's chaplain. The King wanted a place to which he could retreat in prayer and contemplation and also a place where he could be buried, and so gave Cedd land at Lastingham. The Venerable Bede, who visited it in 735, described it as lying among 'mountains, difficult of access and remote, where appeared to be fitter dwelling places for thieves and wild beasts, than for men.'

Here under the directions of Coelin and Cedd a monastery was built and Cedd became its first abbot. The foundation prospered, but in 664 'the yellow plague' swept through the country and struck down Cedd and most of the community. The news of his death so saddened the members of the monasteries which he had established among the East Saxons that 30 of them came to live at Lastingham in order to be near their beloved founder and to be buried close to him.

Shortly before he died Cedd requested that his youngest brother, Chad, himself a holy and devout man, should succeed him as abbot at Lastingham. Chad became Bishop of York and was exemplary in that office. In 669 he resigned and sought the peace and tranquillity of his beloved monastery at Lastingham.

Higher authority, however, had other things in mind for him. When the Bishop of Mercia died, King Wulfhere asked for Chad to be appointed to the bishopric. He favoured Chad because Chad had converted him to Christianity, after he had committed murder.

Wulfhere had two sons, Wulfade and Rufine. One day while out hunting Wulfade chased a stag which sought shelter in a tiny chapel where Chad was leading the life of a hermit. Curious why a man should live this way, Wulfade became intrigued by what Chad had to tell him. He learned the story of Christ and eventually became a Christian and was baptised by Chad. Wulfade told his brother and he too sought instruction from Chad and became converted to Christianity.

One day, while the two brothers were at prayer at Chad's chapel, they were discovered by their father. Furious that they had renounced their pagan rites, he abandoned all reason and, without hesitating, slew his two sons rather than let them follow the new religion. Once his fury had abated, he was filled with remorse. His wife, Ermenilda, her heart torn with grief, begged him to make amends and seek the advice of the hermit on how to accomplish this.

With a heavy heart he sought out Chad, confessed to his crime and was so influenced by the goodness of the man that he received instruction and was converted to Christianity. When Chad left his monastery at Lastingham to become Bishop of Mercia Wulfhere gave him every support and helped to found monasteries within his kingdom. He built a church and dedicated it to St. Mary, the foundation of the present Lichfield Cathedral. He never forgot Lastingham and came there occasionally to pray and meditate. It was there that he hoped to spend his last days, but that was not to be.

One day in February 672 Chad was at prayer in his small chapel at Lichfield. His companion of many years was Ouini, who had joined the community at Lastingham after leaving the court of the Queen of East Anglia. Working outside the chapel, Ouini heard a beautiful sound coming from the heavens. It was as if a choir was descending upon them, but there was no one to be seen. The sound hovered over the chapel where Chad was praying and then it moved inside. Ouini was entranced by the beautiful singing. As it reached a most joyous crescendo it seemed to burst from the chapel, rise into the air, and gradually fade into the distance.

Still frozen in astonishment, Ouini was broken out of his trance by a call from Chad. The holy man bade him go to the church where he knew the seven brethren who formed his community were at prayer. Ouini was to bring them and himself back to Chad's chapel. Chad told them that soon he would be leaving them and that they were to continue their lives in the manner which they had been following, with devotion and love.

When the brethren had returned to the church, Ouini told Chad what he had heard and asked the holy man what it was. Surprised that his companion had also heard the singing, Chad told him that it had been a choir of angels showing him the joys of heaven and telling him that he would experience them in seven days time. Chad commanded Ouini to tell no one what had happened until after he was dead.

Chad died seven days later, and it is said that his soul was taken to heaven by the same angelic choir, accompanied by his beloved brother Cedd. His body was buried at Lichfield far from his beloved monastery at Lastingham, which, alas, was ravaged by the Danes in the 9th century, leaving no traces of that early settlement.

CHAPTER FIVE

CRAYKE, COUNTY DURHAM, YORKSHIRE

In a Directory and Gazetteer of the County of York published in 1823 the following entry appears:

> 'Craike and Craike Castle (in the Bishopric of Durham) though locally situated in the wapentake of Bulmer ... The living is a rectory in the patronage of the Bishopric of Durham ... The freeholders in this place vote for knights for the County of Durham; pleas of land are held in the County of Durham and the jurisdiction of the palatine extends thereto; but in the militia service the legislative thought it expedient to embody the inhabitants with the men of Yorkshire.'

Crayke, to give it its present-day spelling, stands on a small hill, about 12 miles north of York, overlooking the Vale of York and guarding the approaches to the Howardian Hills and the north.

This isolation in the heart of Yorkshire is linked through St. Cuthbert, Bishop of Lindisfarne, with the See of Durham. As a shepherd boy, St. Cuthbert was attracted to the monastic life and joined the abbey founded by St. Aidan on the banks of the Tweed at Melrose. Here he came to love the life and became so attached to the monastery that, years later, when he was sent to the settlement on Lindisfarne, he yearned for the abbey at Melrose. Disturbed that he was not fulfilling his calling on Holy Island, he withdrew to the small island of Farne two miles out in the North Sea. There he lived the life of a hermit. He was called from his retreat to be consecrated a bishop at York, an office which necessitated a great deal of travelling throughout Northumbria. He returned to the monastery of Lindisfarne and to his hermit's life on Farne whenever his public duties allowed.

Egfrid, King of Northumbria, gave the present site of Crayke, and some land around it, to Cuthbert to enable him to establish a monastery where he could pause and rest on his travels. It is likely that one was built, but probably only in the form of mud huts, and excavations have failed to prove its existence in more lasting terms.

St. Cuthbert did not live to carry out his original plan. Realising that his days were numbered, he said farewell to the mainland and to Lindisfarne and returned, for the last time, to his own island of Farne. There he died in March 687 and his body was taken to the church on Lindisfarne. The story of St. Cuthbert does not end there, for even after his death he was not allowed to rest in peace in one place.

Before he died, St. Cuthbert had commanded his monks:

> 'And I would have you know and remember that if necessity compels you to choose one of two evils, I would rather you take my bones from the tomb, carry them with you and, departing from this place, dwell wherever God may ordain than that in any way you should consent to iniquity and put your yoke under the yoke of schismatics.' (Bede's *Life of St. Cuthbert*)

Twice the marauding Danes swept over Lindisfarne, leaving desolation in their wake. In their first, unexpected, hasty retreat, the monks, fleeing for their lives, were forced to leave the body of St. Cuthbert behind, but on returning they found that the raiders had overlooked the Saint's tomb and the body was unmolested.

At the second invasion, in 875, the monks, more prepared for a hasty retreat, carried the coffin with them in their flight and for seven years they wandered through the countryside of northern England with the remains of their beloved monk. In 882 St. Cuthbert's body rested at Crayke for four months before finally being interred in Durham Cathedral.

It is said that the places in which the Saint's body rested became part of the County of Durham, and until 1844, nearly 1,000 years later, Crayke was shown on the map as being part of County Durham, in Yorkshire.

CHAPTER SIX

THE FOUNDING OF JERVAULX

A small band of monks of the order Savigny laboured to create a monastery at Fors near Aysgarth, on land given to them by Acarius Fitz-Bardolf, Lord of Ravensworth, in 1145:

> 'The situation was uncompromising, high in the valley, cold and exposed to fogs, and, therefore, though not unfit for pasturage, ill adapted to the ripening of barley and oats, for wheat was then rarely cultivated even in the low districts north of the Trent.'

Nevertheless the monks toiled to make the best of their lot, hoping and praying that something or someone would come to their aid.

Nor were the monks happy about their relationship with their mother house in France, whose abbot did not agree with the foundation of a new monastery and refused to send more monks to Fors, though it was under his jurisdiction. His attitude did not shake their determination and they asked the Abbot of Byland, still a member of the Order of Savigny at this time, to intercede on their behalf when he attended a general chapter at Savigny.

The outcome of this was that the Abbot of Quarr, in the Isle of Wight, was ordered to visit Fors to determine whether it was a suitable place for a monastery. He ruled against the monks at Fors, but, after all they had gone through, their determination to be independent was fired even further and they refused to abide by the decision.

They put their case before the Abbots of Quarr and Byland, pointing out that:

> 'Within a few years from our first establishment we have now five carucates under the plough, forty cows with their followers, sixteen mares with their foals, the gifts of Earl Conan, five sows with their litters, three hundred sheep, about thirty hides in the tannery, wax and oil which will supply our lights for two years; and we are very certain that we shall be able to raise a competent supply of ale, cheese, bread, and butter, and to sustain a regular convent out of such beginnings, until it shall please God to provide better for them.'

The Abbots listened sympathetically to their plea but delayed their judgement, for at this time there were moves afoot for the Order of Savigny to join the Cistercians. This happened in 1147 and the Abbot of Byland, now that he was a Cistercian, ruled, by the power invested in him, that the Fors monks could act as an independent house and duly appointed John of Kinstan as abbot of the newly independent monastery.

John, with twelve monks, set forth from Byland for their new home, knowing well that they needed a better place in which to dwell, for adverse weather conditions could soon upset the work and bounty achieved at Fors in the past year. As they journeyed John constantly turned the problem over in his mind, for he had the welfare of his little flock at heart and he burned with a desire to raise a monastery and church to the glory of God in a place where his monks could live in peace and dedicate their lives to the service of the Almighty. He prayed that he might be a good abbot while attempting to achieve these objectives.

Asleep on the first night of their journey, John had a troubled dream. He and his monks were in a confined place shut in by briars, thorns and weeds which grew and grew, closing in more and more until the monks were terrified for their lives. The Abbot woke in a terrible fear. What was he leading his monks to? If it was their home he had seen in his dreams, then it was no place to be — but what could he do about it?

He kept his dream and worries to himself as they started out the next morning. He was quiet, keeping himself to himself, and his flock respected his wish, for they saw that he was saying his rosary. A gasp from his companions broke his concentrated thoughts. He was startled by the sight of a beautiful lady standing a short distance ahead of them. A flaxen-haired boy held her hand and in his right hand he held a small branch of a tree. John wondered where they had come from for he was certain that they were not in sight a few moments before, a fact confirmed by his fellow monks, commenting on the sudden appearance of the two strangers.

When he stepped forward, the lady and her boy did not move. He saw friendly smiles and the expression on the lady's face seemed to invite him to tell her what troubled him. That invitation came in words when she asked in the most beautiful, gentlest voice he had ever heard, 'You are worried, my friend. What troubles you?'

Surprised at her perception, the Abbot glanced at the boy. The boy smiled and nodded as if approving his mother's question and encouraged the monk to tell everything:

'Ma'am, we are bound for our tiny dwelling at Fors, to a site which may prove difficult and unsuitable for us to pursue our lives in the service of God.' John went on to tell her more about the site and of his dream the previous night, of how he was certain that it was a sign from God that they needed a different place to live, but that he did not know how to go about finding such a place. The lord had been generous in giving them land in the first instance to so he felt he could not seek their help again.

The lady listened intently and John felt in his outpouring a sense of relief. When he had finished his story the lady smiled a comforting smile and said, 'Do not worry. Follow my son. He will show you a new place where your wishes will be fulfilled.'

Though surprised by this instruction, for how could this young boy show them a place to live, John felt no desire to ridicule.

The boy smiled, held out his hand and said, 'Follow me.'

The Abbot, followed by his monks, started after him, then stopped and turned: 'Dear lady, are you not coming with us?'

'No, my son knows where to take you. Have faith in him.' she replied gently.

'But will he find his way home?' There was concern for the youngster in John's voice.

'Home is in your hearts. I will not lose him,' she replied.

The Abbot hesitated, puzzled, but the lady smiled reassuringly. John turned. The boy seemed to have the confidence of many years in his eyes and John felt his worry disappear.

As they set off, John glanced back. The lady had gone just as mysteriously as she had appeared. He held his council and followed the boy. After traversing some rough ground and battling a way through undergrowth they came to a flat expanse. Though still rough and forbidding, it was less so than the ground they had covered since meeting the lady and her son.

The boy stopped in the middle of this open space. 'This branch I brought from Byland,' he said, a remark which puzzled the monks, for they had not seen the boy there. 'As Byland will prosper like the tree from which I plucked it so too will Jervaulx prosper as this branch grows.' Again the monks were startled, for how could this branch grow? It had no roots.

The boy stooped and pushed the branch into the ground. 'Here it is that God will be adored,' he cried.

The radiant smile on his face as he straightened was infectious, and happiness soared through the tiny band of monks. To their amazement the branch immediately took root and started to grow.

The monks stared in wonder as the tree blossomed and small white birds flew to its branches. Truly they were witnessing a miracle. Remembering the boy, they looked round for him, but he had gone. Immediately the Abbot fell to his knees and offered up a prayer of thanks to the beautiful lady and her son.

The monks at Fors, anxiously awaiting news from Byland, were overjoyed to hear that they had a new home. They hastily packed their few belongings and hurried to join their brethren who, by the time they reached them, had had a visit from Conan, son of the Earl of Richmond. He had shown no surprise at finding the monks at the new and better site. In fact, it was almost as if he had expected their arrival, and he had immediately given the land to them.

CHAPTER SEVEN

THE FOUNDING OF FOUNTAINS

The founding of the great Cistercian abbey of Fountains near Ripon in North Yorkshire, has its roots in St. Mary's Abbey at York, a Benedictine foundation. Benedictine monks, who had been at Lastingham, a wild and desolate place, for eight years, left their monastery, on account of its unsuitable site, and came to York where they founded St. Mary's Abbey in 1088.

The monastery grew in importance but the peaceful life was upset from within when, in 1132, some monks, led by the Prior, Richard, complained that the strict observance of the Rule of St. Benedict was becoming slack. The Abbot of St. Mary's resented the objection of these few monks, seeing it as a complaint against and a threat to his authority. He reminded them of their vow of obedience, but those seeking reform were not to be put off and held to their demand for a stricter rule.

Perhaps they had heard of the Cistercian monks coming to Rievaulx in the same year, 1132, and knew of their stricter interpretation of the Rule of St. Benedict. No matter what it was that sparked off the demands, when they found they were getting nowhere they appealed to Thurstan, the Archbishop of York, for help.

It is in a letter from the Archbishop to the Archbishop of Canterbury, quoted by Hugh of Kirkstall in his Fountains Chronicle of 1270, that we get some idea of the feelings of Prior Richard and his followers in their pursuit of a stricter, more austere life.

> 'For when strife, dissension, and abuse arise among the brethren, and altercations and murmurings against those in authority, it is clear from what kind of root such evil sprang. How then can we be so mad as to call ourselves monks of the blessed Benedict, who forbids with many threats all those things which we in our great presumption are not afraid to do? For these are his own words — "Scandal, and idle talk and jokes we ban everywhere and absolutely; we will not permit a disciple to open his mouth to say such things." And elsewhere he says, "At all times monks ought to aim at silence, but especially in the

night hours." How diligently this decree is observed, everyone knows who has had an opportunity of seeing our habits. For while some of us go into the church after collation, others wander away for trifling and useless chatter, as if the malice of the day were not sufficient unless that of the night were also added. And why recall our extravagance in diet? For many dishes are added over and above what was ordered by the blessed Benedict, giving the wicked impression that the rule is best observed where the greatest superfluity can be enjoyed. Why should I speak of our exquisite delicacies, our variously flavoured sauces, our many dainties? Assuredly new stimulation is applied to the full and over-gorged belly, so that, while there is hardly a scrap of room left in it, the voluptuous desire of eating still grows. And though the burdened lungs belch forth intolerable stinks, a new variety of food removes satiety. The same is true of the agreeable and splendid variety of drinks, of the elaborate delicacy of raiment. These were not the sentiments or the teachings of our blessed Benedict, according to whose rule we make our profession. For the rule looks at warmth, not colour in dress; it seeks not to savour in the articles of food, but satisfies necessity with a frugal diet.'

Such was the basis of the complaints Prior Richard and his band raised with their abbot and on which he took no action, resulting in Richard appealing to the Archbishop.

Thurstan could not ignore the complaint and duly arranged a visitation to St. Mary's Abbey, where he proposed the matter could be discussed. On 6 October 1132, Thurstan with his retinue of authoritative clergy arrived at the abbey only to find that the Abbot had gathered learned monks in considerable numbers to oppose the Archbishop's entry.

Thurstan's insistant demands to be admitted to the Chapter House for consultation were met with equally ferocious refusals from the Abbot. Pandemonium and tumult raged as rival factions each loudly proclaimed their rights. The dissident monks managed to align themselves alongside the Archbishop and his supporters, and, once the tumult had died down, Thurstan escorted the 13 would-be reformers from the monastery and gave them shelter within his own buildings.

The Abbot, annoyed that his authority had been flouted, was determined to have his wayward monks, as he saw them, back under his jurisdiction. Accordingly he went to higher authority, writing and stating his case to the King and influential Church authorities. Archbishop Thurstan, anticipating the Abbot's reactions, wrote at length to the Archbishop of Canterbury, who was also the Papal Legate, recording the events which had taken place and pleading the case of his dissenters.

The monks were allowed to stay under the care of the Archbishop, and at the end of three months, at Christmas 1132, he took them to Ripon where he had some land which he gave to them. Their hearts must have despaired on seeing the site for, according to *An Eccesiastical History of Yorkshire* written by Dr. Burton in 1757:

> 'The spot of ground had never been inhabited unless by wild beasts, being overgrown with wood and brambles, lying between two steep hills and rocks, covered with wood on all sides, more proper for a retreat of wild beasts than the human species; this was called Skell-dale, that is the vale of Skel, a rivulet running through it ... they withdrew into this uncouth desert, without any house to shelter them in that winter season, or provisions to subsist on, but entirely depended on the divine providence.'

And yet there must have been a certain joy in their hearts for this was what they wanted — a chance to lead a stricter mode of life, interpreting the Rule of St. Benedict as they saw it, in all its frugality and strictness.

Hugh of Kirkstall in *The Fountains Chronicle* of 1207 recalls their first winter:

> 'There was an elm in the middle of the valley...Here the holy men gathered to seek shelter in its shade...they lay around it, keeping off the harsh winter as best they could with straw and grasses thrown over them ... They all slept under the one tree, all sat at meals under the one tree, a poor convent but strong in the Lord; twelve priests and one deacon. The holy bishop served their bread, the stream flowing nearby their drink.'

They survived that harsh first winter and during it started to clear and till the ground with the hope of erecting some buildings, the beginnings of a new monastery. They elected as abbot Richard, the Prior of St. Mary's Abbey in York, who had led them in their cause.

Because they wished to lead a stricter life than they had followed at York they applied to transfer from the Benedictine order, of which they were still members, to the Cistercians. Their letter to Bernard, the Abbot of Clairvaux, who had sent monks to found Cistercian monasteries in England, was backed by word from Archbishop Thurstan. Bernard viewed their case sympathetically and corresponded with all parties involved, and finally agreed to them becoming Cistercians. He sent Geoffrey, a monk of his monastery, to instruct them in the Cistercian way of life.

They were joined by 17 new recruits and, while this was a case for rejoicing, it did present the unestablished monastery with more problems for there were more mouths to feed and more accommodation was needed.

Hugh of Kirkstall tells us:

'And it happened, after some days, that hunger grew strong in our area and the holy men were severely pressed. There were no loaves to eat, no money to buy them, no harvest in the granaries, and a considerable mass of poor people flowed in their direction. The Abbot went around the places nearby asking food for the brothers, and there was no-one to give it to them nor did anyone have the means to provide it. There was privation everywhere. To stay in one place was grim enough; to stay there, lonely and without food, completely impossible. Driven at last to the extremes of poverty, they stripped the leaves from the trees, gathered simple country herbs and, adding a little salt, cooked rations...'

The lean time through which the small community went was so disheartening that in 1134, their abbot, Richard, attending the General Chapter of the Cistercian Order at Citeaux, asked Abbot Bernard to find a more hospitable site, somewhere in France, to which they could move their monastery. Bernard did so, but nothing was finalised until Richard had returned and consulted his monks at Fountains.

However, when Richard reached home he found the situation had changed. The Dean of York, old and in poor health, had decided that he should spend his remaining years as a member of the community at Fountains. Following the Cistercian rule, his considerable fortune was divided into three parts, one third for building and maintenance, one for general purposes appertaining to the monastery and one for the poor. With financial worries lifted from their shoulders, the monks could establish their monastery on a firm and lasting basis.

Archbishop Thurstan now legally conveyed the land to the monks and the foundation of Fountains was assured.

CHAPTER EIGHT

THE HUNTER'S DEATH

Great joy came to Walter Espec, Lord of Helmsley, and his wife, Adeline, with the birth of their son. They christened him Walter, after his father, and took delight in watching him grow under their inspired guidance into a fine young man. He took a keen interest in his father's estates, loved hunting, was a fine horseman and adept with all manner of weapons. He was indeed the apple of their eyes and their extensive wealth was as nothing compared to their love for their son.

One morning all was bustle around their home. Retainers prepared horses, weapons for the hunt were checked, and young Walter laughed and joked with the friends he had invited to hunt with him. His father watched the preparations, wishing he could spare the time to accompany the party this fine day on what promised to be an exhilarating hunt. Adeline, who had been watching the activities from a window, was struck by a strange feeling. It was as if a cold hand had touched her heart. Her face drained of its colour and she steadied herself against the wall as all strength drained from her. Though the sun was still shining, the day seemed grey and dismal. She gazed at the scene below as if it was a tiny tableau being enacted before her. A desire to stop it was strong and yet she felt helpless to do so. Her mind fought to overcome the barrier and suddenly she broke through, turned from the window and hurried to the courtyard.

As she came into the bright sunlight everything was back to normal, but the deep premonition, dark and foreboding, was still with her. Her husband welcomed her with a warm loving smile but she hurried past him to her son who had just mounted his horse still held by one of the servants. Walter, in the best of spirits, greeted her heartily with love and admiration, but he was troubled when he noticed the usual affection in his mother's eyes was clouded with misgiving.

Before he could question her, her plea to him not to go hunting was made with all the passion she could muster. She told him of her premonition of impending disaster but Walter laughed it off. When she insisted, he asked her if the disaster had anything to do with the hunt and Adeline had to admit that she did not know, only that the forewarning had come to her while she had watched the preparations from the window.

31

Her husband had come forward and, though he always placed great store by his wife's wisdom and reasoning, he could see nothing to prevent the hunt taking place. Walter reassured his mother that it had only been a feeling and that it did not mean anything. Besides it was such a fine day and he could not disappoint his friends, whom he had invited to the hunt. Without any more ado Walter threw his mother a kiss, gave her a broad uplifting smile and led his party off.

The hunt went well. The horseman ranged far. Walter and his friends enjoyed themselves, each trying to outdo the other, yet with the adventurous caution of the hunter. Their laughter and cajoling sounded on the summer air. The zest of youth, entwined in high spirits, led the riders on until, late in the day, they found themselves close to the River Derwent, about six miles from the old Roman town of Derventio. They had decided to call it a day and Walter smiled to himself as he recalled his mother's premonition of tragedy. If it referred to anything it certainly wasn't to himself or the hunt. Now they would enjoy a gentle ride home while the setting sun coloured the hills with ever-changing hues casting shadows across the Derwent.

Walter sent his horse forward. Suddenly a wild boar, startled by the nearness of unwanted intruders, and, sensing danger, sprang from some bushes close to the hooves of Walter's horse. Frightened by the unexpected disturbance and the presence of a dangerous animal, the horse reared in confusion. Caught unawares, Walter was thrown from his mount. It had happened to him before and he had never been the worse for it. But this time alarm ran through the party when they saw he did not move. His companions were quickly at his side and horror chilled their hearts and numbed their minds when they saw that Walter was dead, the gash on his head, where he had hit an ancient stone cross, telling its tale of doom.

With heavy hearts and deep sadness the tragic party wended its way home where, somehow knowing that her premonition had been fulfilled, Adeline waited, with her husband by her side, to receive the dead body of her beloved son. The parents were grief stricken but they faced the tragedy of losing their heir bravely. Walter, a good and religious man, found some solace in the advice of his uncle, an Augustinian monk at Nostell Priory, who suggested that Walter make Christ his heir.

Walter took this to heart and in 1132 built a religious house for the Augustinians at Kirkham, where his beloved son had been killed, so that his death should not be in vain. He also gave some of his lands to found Wardon Abbey in Bedfordshire about 1135 and had already given land to the Cistercians to establish an abbey at Rievaulx where, in later years, he lived as a monk until his death.

CHAPTER NINE

THE OUTWITTING OF THE ABBOT OF ST. MARY'S

'It's time we ate,' suggested Little John as Robin Hood and his men lingered in the forest on one of their visits to Yorkshire.

'Aye, thee's right, big fellow,' agreed Friar Tuck, patting his huge stomach and relishing the thought of some juicy meat.

A murmur of agreement came from the rest of the band but Robin silenced them. 'We'll eat, lads, but only when we have some baron, knight, squire, abbot or bishop to pay for it. Off with thee, Little John, Will and Mutch. See who ye can find, no harm mind thee, but bring him here to dine and lodge with us and pay for the feast.'

A chuckle went round the men from Sherwood for Robin had worked this plan before and it had always resulted in a worthy feast at no expense, for the 'guest', afraid of what might happen, was only too willing to pay the cost. Little John, Will Scarlet and Mutch, the miller's son, headed for the main trackway through the forest and there lay in waiting for a victim.

After only a short while they heard the clop of a slowly ridden horse. They exchanged puzzled glances, surprised that there was not more urgency about the rider. A few moments later a knight rode into sight, but a sorrier looking knight they had never seen. His clothes were dirty and unkempt, he drooped in the saddle, his hood was askew and hung over his face. There was about him an air of despondency, as if he had all the troubles in the world on his shoulders and he had given up trying to cope with them.

The three men doubted if such a figure could meet their requirements but Robin had said the first person who filled one of the categories he had named. After all, he was a knight and his appearance did not necessarily match the money he might be carrying. He may even have adopted this look to throw would-be robbers off the scent.

John nodded to his two companions and as one they broke cover.

'Good day to you, good knight,' called Little John, stepping a couple of paces in front of his friends.

The knight raised his head and, seeing his progress barred, halted his horse.

'Welcome to the forest,' went on Little John. 'My master and his men are about to eat but he would not sit down to feast without some stranger join us. Thee's come along so thee must be our guest. What sayest thou?'

Surprised by this unusual bidding, the knight hesitated but, seeing a friendliness in the men confronting him, asked with a touch of suspicion in his voice. 'Who is thy master?'

A likeable man, good sir. A noble man, though outlawed to the forest by unjust accusations from treacherous Norman lords. His name, sir, is Robin Hood.' Little John gave the information with a stirring pride at being a companion of Robin's.

'Ah, I have heard of the fellow, good things and bad.' The knight's melancholy look was accompanied by a resigned shrug of the shoulders. 'I shall accompany thee and see for myself, though I suspect I have no choice in the matter.'

He turned his horse to follow Will and Mutch while Little John fell into step beside him.

As they made their way through the forest Little John realised, from the depressed expression on the knight's face and the sadness in his eyes, that something of importance was troubling him. His curiosity nearly got the better of him and he only drew back from questioning the knight as the words came to his lips. It was no concern of his and he knew that Robin would elicit the information if he felt he had cause to do so. Otherwise the man's private affairs were his own.

When Robin saw his men and the knight approaching their glade in the forest, he came forward to greet his visitor. His curiosity was aroused when he saw the state of the stranger and sensed the melancholy air about him.

Robin hid his surprise, and his men, taking the hint from their leader, did likewise.

'Welcome to the forest, good sir.' greeted Robin, bowing a courteous welcome to the stranger. 'We have waited for someone to share our feast, so come, good knight, you are most welcome.'

The knight nodded and swung from his horse. 'I thank thee, Robin Hood. It is goodly kind of thee.' He glanced at the feast spread out in the glade and his eyes widened in astonishment. Never had he imagined such an array of food could be assembled in the forest. 'By my oath, I have not eaten such fare for many a long day,' he said with a glance at Robin.

'Then thou shalt enjoy it,' laughed Robin. 'Will, take this good knight, see that he is refreshed after his ride, and then bring him to his place beside me.'

As the knight accompanied Will Scarlet, Robin turned to Little John. 'This fellow looks as if he has come on hard times. What thinkest thou?'

'He gave me no inkling, Robin, but his appearance holds out your idea,' replied Little John. 'And as well as melancholia there is a sadness about him which touches me deep.'

'I've noticed that too but maybe it's an act to fool us into thinking he has nothing worth taking.' Robin rubbed his chin thoughtfully. 'Yet there is an air of good breeding, a distinguished look behind that sadness. We shall see.'

When the knight returned, the feast began and the whole band fell to with real enjoyment, none more so than the knight.

When the final morsel had been taken, the knight turned to Robin. 'That indeed was a feast fit for a king. It's one I will never forget.'

'Indeed it is not,' replied Robin with a mischievous twinkle in his eyes, 'for now thou must pay for it!'

The knight stiffened. His eyes darkened. 'What? You say this to a guest!'

'I say this to a knight,' went on Robin. 'If thou remember, a poor outlaw does not pay for a knight's meal, rather it is the custom for the knight to make the payment.'

'Trickery, my good Robin, thou hast delved into trickery.' The knight raised his hand when he saw that Robin would speak. 'But hold on a moment, If what thou sayest is that thee expects me to pay, thou will be disappointed for all I have in this world is ten shillings.'

Robin laughed in disbelief and a murmur went round his band signalling that they all thought this stranger was trying to deceive them.

'Thou can laugh, but it is true,' went on the knight.

Robin's eyes sharpened. 'Then thou will have no objection to Little John testing the truth of thy words.'

'None whatsoever. Here is my purse.' The knight tossed it to Little John who caught it deftly and poured its contents on to the palm of his broad left hand. Ten shillings was all that nestled there.

Robin looked at the knight. 'And you've none hidden anywhere else on your person or on your horse?'

The unflinching way in which the knight met his gaze and the sincerity in his voice when he said, 'I have nothing more,' convinced Robin that he was telling the truth.

'Then I shall take nothing from thee.' He nodded to Little John, who slid the coins back into the purse and handed it back to its owner.

'Now, good knight, fill thy horn with more wine and tell me how you come on hard times. No money, ill clad and yet, behind your stooped shoulders, behind the cares which hang heavy round your neck, I detect a once proud and noble lord, a man of authority.' -

The knight sighed. 'Indeed you are right, Robin. Hard times have struck and there are harder to come for Sir Richard of Lea.'

'Sir Rich...Thou art Sir Richard of Lea?' gasped Robin.

'I am,' replied the knight.'

'Then I know of thee. I've heard tell of the acres of land thou own in Yorkshire.'

'Did own, Robin, *did* own,' Sir Richard pointed out sadly.

Robin frowned. 'What meanest thou, Sir Richard?'

'I was on my way to a meeting with the Abbot of St. Mary's Abbey when your fellows stopped me. And right glad I am they did. I feel much better after that feast but, sadly, it cannot alter the outcome of my meeting, the forfeiture of all my lands, and so with them I'll lose four hundred pounds a year income and have nothing on which to support my wife and children.'

'What!' Robin gasped with astonishment and a murmur, tinged with surprise and sympathy, ran through the band of men who had been listening intently to Sir Richard. 'But why to the Abbot, a man I know to be greedy where the wealth of his abbey of York is concerned. A man who even takes from the poor on the pretext that giving will save their souls. But tell me, Sir Richard, how thee has come into the clutches of such a man?'

'Alas, my eldest son killed a knight of Lancaster,' explained Sir Richard. 'It was in fair fight but there were those who did not see it that way and had him brought to trial. To save him I had to sell all my goods and mortgage my lands to the Abbot of St. Mary's.'

'To what price did thou mortgage?' asked Robin.

'Four hundred pounds.'

Robin gave a low whistle. 'A year's income. And if thou doest not pay thou lose all your lands.' Robin looked thoughtful. 'I expect at this moment the Abbot and his monks will be rejoicing gleefully, thinking that thou aren't coming with money and the land will be theirs.'

'I expect they are,' agreed Sir Richard sadly. 'And they'll rejoice all the more when I do arrive and tell them that I do not have the four hundred pounds.'

'Then let us give them a shock,' grinned Robin.

A puzzled frown creased Sir Richard's brow. 'What meanest thou?'

'Thee will pay them in full,' replied Robin.

'But how can I?' returned Sir Richard, irritated by Robin's apparent lack of understanding. 'I've told you, all I have is ten shillings. Thee's seen it for thyself.'

Robin raised his voice, 'Shall we lend it to him, lads?'

'Aye.' With one voice, the men of Sherwood approved.

'But ...' Sir Richard, lost for words, stared at Robin.

'There you are, we'll let you have it,' said Robin. He turned to Little John. 'Fetch it, big fellow.'

'Right away,' cried Little John, delighted that Robin had seen fit to help this knight to whom he had taken a liking. As he moved away he indicated to Will Scarlet to accompany him.

A few minutes later the two men were back, Little John with the money and Will carrying a new outfit.

'Thou shalt not appear before this abbot looking as you do. Don these new clothes and ride with pride,' said Robin.

Sir Richard took the clothes with grateful thanks and, when he reappeared after he had changed, there was a new bearing about him. He was a man proud to bear a knight's arms, proud to be Sir Richard of Lea, a man of means and property.

'The money, Sir Richard,' said Robin holding out a pouch. 'Take it with all our best wishes.' He laughed. 'I'd like to see the Abbot's face when you present it to him. Ah, but I'll get a first-hand report. A knight cannot ride without a squire in attendance, so Little John will fill that role and walk with thee. Just one thing more.' Robin looked beyond his men and raised his arm. At the signal Mutch led a powerful, well-groomed steed towards them.

Sir Richard gasped. He turned to Robin. 'I will never be able to repay your kindness and generosity, but I will repay the money, and, as I ride to an abbey dedicated to Our Lady, she shall be my surety. Just say the time and the place and I'll be there with it.'

'I can have no better surety for I have a special devotion to Our Lady, and I'm certain She will see that I am repaid, so let's say a year from today in this very place,' replied Robin.

'Truly I will be here to repay thee in full,' cried Sir Richard. He took Robin's hand in a warm grip and grasped his shoulder as he would a brother.

'Away with thee, Sir Richard,' cried Robin, 'Thou has an important mission to wipe the smirk off the face of that greedy abbot.'

Sir Richard mounted his horse and raised his hand, acknowledging the good luck shouts from the men of the greenwood as he rode out of the glade.

On his return Little John had to recount his story over and over again for the amusement or Robin and his men, of how Sir Richard had feigned his inability to pay, of how he had pleaded to be given more time, of how the Abbot had refused, taking pleasure in having the knight at his mercy, of how he, his prior and cellarer gloated over the extension of their lands and the riches they would bring, of their astonishment when Sir Richard produced the money in full and retrieved the forfeiture of his lands, of how they squirmed under the chastisement meted out by Sir Richard for their hardness, greed and uncharitable attitude.

A year later Robin, having recalled that this was the day when Sir Richard should repay his debt, awaited his coming. A feast had been prepared pending Sir Richard's arrival, but, with the sun lowering towards the west, doubts were beginning to creep into Robin's mind.

'It looks as though Our Lady is not pleased with me,' said Robin.

'There is still time,' pressed Little John. 'The sun has not set yet. Sir Richard is an honourable man. I'd stake my life on it. Besides Our Lady was his surety and I'm sure he would not want to fail her.'

'Thy faith is greater than mine, good fellow,' replied Robin. 'But see the feast is ready. It shall not be wasted. Go, thee and Will and Mutch, and bring some guest to share it.'

Little John, Will Scarlet and Mutch, the miller's son, hastened to the spot where they had first met Sir Richard. They had been there only a few minutes when they heard a body of horsemen and retinue of footmen approaching. From their hiding place they spied three monks riding fine steeds, accompanied by several guards on horseback and a number of armed footmen.

'Three simple monks with a following that befits a bishop,' chuckled Little John. 'I think we have a prize here, lads.'

'But there are too many of them and we are but three,' pointed out Mutch cautiously.

'Aye, we are but we have surprise,' returned Little John. 'Keep your arrows pointed at the hearts of the monks. Thee, Will, the one on the left, Mutch, thee the one on the right. Leave the one in the middle for me.'

To gain a better advantage he held them back a moment longer and in that measure of time he recognised the holy men.

'Oh, this is a better prize than I thought,' grinned Little John. 'We have for our guests none other than the Abbot of St. Mary's, his Prior and Cellarer.'

'What!' gasped Will. 'Thee's sure?'

'As sure as I crouch in this undergrowth,' replied Little John. They are the very three whom Sir Richard faced when I accompanied him to St. Mary's.' Little John eyed the approaching party. 'Now!' he whispered.

In that instant the three men stepped on to the trackway, their bows ready, their arrows pointing at the very hearts of the monks. The surprise was complete. Confusion reigned among the escort at finding the track barred by three armed men.

Before any semblance of order returned, Little John shouted, 'Hold thy men back, good monks.' There was a derisory note in the way he emphasised the word good. 'Our arrows point directly at thy hearts! Death is thine should anyone move towards us.'

The leading monk held up his hands, forbidding any of his retinue to move against these men. 'Who is thou and what doest thee want?' he demanded haughtily, showing contempt for the man who confronted him. 'We have nothing thee could want. We are but poor monks.'

'Poor?' Little John gave a derisory laugh. 'With a following like this? Besides, since when was an abbot poor?'

Startled, the Abbot looked askance at Little John but immediately regained his composure. 'Nevertheless, I travel with little.'

'Enough of this,' snapped Little John. 'My master awaits you to dine with him.'

'Dine?' The Abbot was puzzled by this change of attitude. 'Who is thy master?'

'Robin Hood.'

There was a touch of fear mixed with the astonishment which flicked the Abbot's eyes. The Prior and Cellarer exchanged glances of alarm, and a murmur, toned with anxiety, ran through the armed escort.

'Send thy men away, abbot,' Little John raised his voice. 'And none of thee turn back. Make no attempt to follow us. There are good men and true with their arrows pointing at thee from their hiding places. They'll drop thee if thee doest not leave this place. And we hold thy abbot's life in forfeit.'

The Abbot signalled to his retinue to do as they were told.

The bluff had worked and, as the escort started to move away, Little John ordered the pack horse to be left behind and the leading reins to be handed to the Prior and the Cellarer who were astonished that this man should know their monastic office. They were still puzzling over this when they reached the glade in the forest. Robin came forward to greet the new-found guests.

'Ah, Little John, thee found someone to dine with us,' he cried.

'I did, good Robin,' smiled Little John. 'None other than the Abbot of St. Mary's, his Prior and Cellarer. Me thinks Our Lady has not deserted thee.'

'We shall see,' said Robin, 'but come, let us eat.'

The men from the abbey were escorted to their places and, enjoying their food and wine, some of the hostility and suspicion fell from them.

'Now, Lord Abbot,' said Robin when the feasting had finished and the Abbot started to take his leave, 'before thee go, thee must pay. Thee know that it would not be fitting for an outlaw to pay for the repast taken by an abbot and his fellow monks of authority: rather it should be the other way round.'

'But I thought we were your guests,' replied the Abbot indignantly.

'That was a misapprehension under which you laboured,' replied Robin.

'Well, I'm afraid thee will be disappointed. We are a poor community and we have nought but ten shillings with us.'

'If that be the case,' said Robin, 'then I will not take anything from thee, but if thee lie then I take the lot. Now, thee will not mind if we search your possessions.'

Protestations sprang to the Abbot's lips but he realised it was useless to do so.

Robin nodded to Little John who together with Will and Mutch emptied all the contents of the Abbot's purse and from the pack horses onto a cloak which they had spread on the ground. When they had finished there lay coins and silver to the value of eight hundred pounds.

'Well, thou tried to trick me, Abbot.' Robin's face darkend with anger. 'For that I take everything.'

Red faced, his temper boiling, the Abbot started to protest.

'I see this as the work of Our Lady,' cut in Robin. 'She has sent thee to repay a debt incurred a year ago.'

'Debt?' boomed the Abbot, trying to gain the initiative from Robin.

'Aye,' rasped Robin. 'I loaned a good knight four hundred pounds a year ago to be brought to thee at thy Abbey, otherwise thee in thy greed would take all his land and possesions. He took it with Our Lady as surety. He was to repay me today but Our Lady has sent thee instead.'

'Thee talks nonsense,' snapped the Abbot. 'I know of no such debt.'

'Thou liest!' Little John stepped forward. 'I was there when the money was handed over to thee. Thou sayest thee are Our Lady's servant. She must have sent thee to repay the debt and it looks as though it is with interest.

'Truly Our Lady smiles on us,' agreed Robin. 'She is the truest woman I have ever found. No, pray good monks, be on your way. No harm shall come to thee.'

The men of Sherwood helped the monks prepare to leave and escorted them back to the trail, where they left them to contemplate on the reversal of their fortunes.

When Robin's men reached the glade in the forest they found their leader looking somewhat melancholy in spite of the fact that their debt had been more than repaid.

'What ails thee, Robin?' queried Little John.

'Well, the debt has been repaid and Our Lady must favour me, but I am disappointed that Sir Richard is not a man of his word.'

'There may be many reasons why he has not come.' pointed out Little John, 'and the fact that the Abbot of St. Mary's came this way, bearing more than sufficient money, on this very day must have been the workings of Our Lady on behalf of Sir Richard.'

Robin nodded, but, before he could make a remark, the sound of a horse brought a cautious alertness to the band of men.

A few moments later Sir Richard of Lea came into view. Robin, his melancholia and doubts suddenly gone, sprang forward to greet him.

'Good Sir Richard, truly I'm glad to see thee.'

'And I thee, Robin.'

Sir Richard swung from his horse and the two men clasped hands in a grip of everlasting friendship.

'I'm late, thou must have doubted me,' cried Sir Richard. 'But I'm here, a year to the day as I promised. And here I have for thee the four hundred pounds thee loaned me.' Sir Richard held out a purse. 'And there's twenty pound more for your generosity.'

'Nay, gracious knight, I have already been repaid,' said Robin.

'Thee's been repaid?' Sir Richard frowned unable to comprehend how this could be so.

'Aye,' replied Robin. 'Our Lady was the surety and she sent the Abbot of St. Mary's with the money. More than that, with interest she doubled it!'

Sir Richard gaped at Robin in astonishment.

Robin laughed. 'I shall explain while we drink a horn of wine together and thou partake of what is left of our feast.'

Sir Richard enjoyed the tale and how the Abbot of St. Mary's had been outwitted by Robin and particularly by Our Lady.

'But see, Sir Richard, I have got my money back so I do not need what thee hast brought me. Thou must keep that and thou shalt have the interest too, for, after all, it was thy money which the Abbot was keeping safe for thee.'

Though Sir Richard protested, Robin would have none of it.

'Then, whenever thou art in these parts thee and thy men shall be my guests and will always have my protection.'

'Thanks, Sir Richard, and if ever thou art in need of money again come to Robin Hood for we seem to be able to make a profit together.'

CHAPTER TEN

THE PURSUIT OF A VISION

The founding of Selby Abbey came about through two men, vastly different in character and in their station in life — William the Conqueror and Benedict, a monk of the Benedictine monastery at Auxerre in France. About 1068 Benedict had a vision of St. Germain who had been made Bishop of Auxerre in 428. Benedict tried to find an answer to the question, 'Why had St. Germain appeared to me?', and wondered if the answer lay in the life of this holy man.

He studied the saint's life closely and found him to be a devout man, ruling his bishopric with kindness and understanding. In 429 he had been sent by Pope Celestine I to Britain to put down the Pelagian heresy. He was accompanied by the Bishop of Troyes and they were successful in this, confounding the Pelagians' beliefs at a meeting at St. Albans. The two bishops returned home but, after a minor outbreak in 447, St. Germain was sent to Britain again to quell the heresy. Once more he was triumphant, returned home and died at Ravenna in 448. He was taken to Auxerre for burial.

The unusual aspects of the saint's life were his two visits to Britain, and Benedict wondered if that was the sign he was looking for. Was he meant to go there? Would he find the landscape, which had formed the background to his vision, there? The more he thought about it the more convinced he became that he was being directed to Britain and that it was there that he would fulfil his religious destiny. Benedict was granted permission to leave the monastery at Auxerre and come to Britain. His abbot gave him his blessing and also a mummified finger of Saint Germain.

After landing on the south coast, Benedict started his search for the place in his vision. He travelled north, alert to the fact that round the next corner he might find his place of destiny. He moved, always with a trust in the Lord and a belief that he would be guided by St. Germain. Accordingly he found himself boarding a ship in King's Lynn, a fact, now that he was in Britain, which would have puzzled him had he not learned that the vessel was bound for the ports along the Humber and the River Ouse. Feeling that he must have been guided by St. Germain to take this ship, he kept a sharp look out for the scene which had filled his mind ever since that special day in

Auxerre. Slowly the ship made its way along the wide Humber and followed the twisting Ouse. The river narrowed and Benedict knew that soon the voyage would be at its limit at York. Maybe he was destined to disembark there and continue his search on foot.

He fought off disappointment and despair for those feelings had no part in a man who trusted in God's will and in the power of St. Germain to achieve it. Commands cut through the gentle breeze as the captain skilfully brought the vessel to a tiny quay at the small settlement at Selby. Benedict watched and admired the brawn and dexterity of the crew as he had done on numerous other occasions since leaving King's Lynn.

As he leaned on the rail, his gaze turned to the scene beside the settlement. Startled, he straightened and he began to tremble with excitement. There it was, the scene in his vision! His eyes widened, taking in the view. Yes! The river bank in the foreground, meadows, with tree-lined ditches, stretching beyond, to the left some huts. This was it, this was where he was meant to be. But why? He could see nothing there which could explain St. Germain's call. Nevertheless this was the place. This is where he must leave the ship. He hurriedly gathered his few belongings and, with thanks, bade farewell to the captain and his crew.

Curious glances were cast in his direction, for rarely did a ship bring a passenger to their tiny settlement. He smiled and nodded to people going about their business as he walked from the quay, his eyes alert for some clue as to why he had been guided here. His footsteps took him beside the river with large open meadows on his left. The day was fine with a sun shining from a blue sky mottled with white fluffy clouds moving slowly in the gentle breeze. Birds sang and fish were jumping in the river.

The sharp clatter of wings intruded into his thoughts. He glanced to his right and saw three swans about to land on the water. They touched down simultaneously and stopped, their positions forming the points of a triangle. Benedict stared. The swans held their places. Three of them. A triangle — the Holy Trinity. The sign he had wanted. Here he must build a church to the glory of God. He made himself a rough shelter and settled there under the questioning gaze of the local people. Word spread that he wished to create a religious settlement, and a few other men wishing to devote their lives to God joined him.

This small religious community which was established beside the tiny settlement of lay-folk came to the notice of Hugh, Sheriff of York. He offered the monks help but, because they were on royal ground, took them to meet King William who at that time was in York. William regarded himself as a champion of the Church and saw the advantage of linking this with his political aspirations. If he gave permission to these men and helped them to establish a monastery in this part of the country, it would not only show his tolerance and generosity after the devasting Harrying of the North, but it would also influence and strengthen the district's loyalty to him and thereby set an example to the rest of the country.

Accordingly he gave land to Benedict and his followers on which they could build a monastery, with Benedict as their first abbot. The significance of the three swans alighting on the river in front of Benedict has never been forgotten, for they appear on Selby Abbey's coat of arms.

CHAPTER ELEVEN

YOUNG EGREMOND

'There is not to be found in England a tract of land more beautiful than the vale of Bolton. Rich in fertile meadows, adorned with noble trees and deep, retiring woodland with long vistas of brown river hastening through. The ruined Priory and Abbey Church, the ancient gateway, surrounded by an amphitheatre of hills enclosing a scene beautiful beyond description, teeming with historical interest.'

So wrote Edmund Bogg, a Yorkshire writer. The Bolton he refers to is Bolton Abbey in Wharfedale. The 'brown river' is the Wharfe and the fact that it hastens at this point is due to being hemmed in by rocks. It narrows so much that the water rushes through with great turbulence.

In his *History of Craven* written in 1803 Dr. T.D. Whitaker says:

'The Wharfe suddenly contracts itself to a rocky channel little more than four feet wide, and pours through the tremendous fissure with a rapidity proportioned to its confinement. This place was then, as it is still, called the Strid, from a feat often excercised by persons of more agility than prudence, who stride from brink to brink, regardless of the destruction which awaits a faltering step.'

The Strid and the Priory, for the monastery was never an abbey even though the settlement takes the name of Bolton Abbey, are bound together in the legend about the founding of the Priory.

In 1120 William Meschin and his wife, Cecilia de Rumilly, founded a priory for Augustinian monks at Embsay about five miles west of Bolton. The land proved unsuitable and Alice de Rumilly, William's and Cecilia's daughter, a widow, who had inherited the estates, looked for a more suitable place.

Alice's son, Romilly, 'the Boy of Egremond', for he had been born at Egremond Castle in Cumbria, was a lively, adventurous youth who loved the outdoor life. One day, when staying at Bolton, he went out with his favourite hound, accompanied by a retainer who knew the area.

As they looked for deer their footsteps took them to the Strid. Excitement stirred in the youth as he viewed the waters roaring through the chasm 30 feet below. He glanced across the cleft and judged it to be little more than four feet to the other side. To cross it would save a long walk and, besides, there was a touch of adventure to stride across those pounding waters. Before the forester could warn him of the danger or fling out a hand to stop him, young Romilly strode purposefully forward and leaped as he had done many times before. The hound, held on a leash, moving beside him, suddenly took fright and, as the boy jumped, held back. The leash tightened, jerked at his master's wrist and threw him out of his stride. He fell short of the opposite side and plunged to his death among the rocks in the wildly surging waters.

The retainer ran to the brink and, with a cold heart, his body numb with the horror of the disaster, stared into the deadly depths. The body had gone, swept away in the roaring tumult. He stood, the tossing waters mocking his hope that somehow the boy had survived. Slowly he turned away, cursing the scene of the disaster, damning the Strid which had taken so young a life, robbing the valley of the cries and laughter of a youth whose zest for life had been infectious.

With hunched shoulders and leadened feet he traced his steps back to the Lady Alice, who knew from his appearance that something was wrong. With a heavy heart the good servant broke the tragic news. Shocked, numb with grief, the mother cried, but in her tears she resolved that some good should come out of the tragedy. She would build a memorial to her son close to the point of his death and that memorial would be a new home for the monks at Embsay.

Fact, however, proves that there is no substance in that legend, for the boy was signatory, along with his mother, to the document giving land to the monks of Bolton. But often legend has some substance within it, and it is likely that Cecilia, Alice's mother, lost a son this way.

Whatever the truth, the legend attracted the interest of William Wordsworth, who was friendly with the Rev. William Carr, rector of the church converted from the Priory nave.

In his ballad, *The Force of Prayer*, Wordsworth writes:

'Young Romilly through Barden woods
  Is ranging high and low;
  And holds a greyhound in a leash,
  To let slip upon buck or doe.

'The pair have reached that fearful chasm,
  How tempting to bestride!
  For lordly Wharfe is there pent in
  With rocks on either side.

The striding-place is called THE STRID,
  A name which it took of yore:

A thousand years hath it borne that name,
And shall a thousand more.

And hither is young Romilly come,
And what may now forbid
That he, perhaps for the hundreth time,
Shall bound across THE STRID?

He sprang in glee, for what cared he
That the river was strong, and the rocks were steep?
But the greyhound in the leash hung back,
And checked him in his leap.

The Boy is in the arms of Wharf,
And strangled by a merciless force;
For never more was young Romilly seen
Till he rose a lifeless corpse.

Long, long in darkness did she sit,
And her first words were, "Let there be
In Bolton, on the field of Wharf,
A stately Priory!"'

CHAPTER TWELVE

AELRED AND THE NOVICE

A young Cistercian novice, Simon, had doubts about his vocation. His mind wrestled with the problem: should he continue his life as a monk, a calling which he had felt strongly but on which he was now having second thoughts, or should he return to the outside world, to a life which had been sweet and enjoyable in spite of some problems and hardships? But those hardships were nothing compared to those he had to endure in the great Cistercian monastery of Rievaulx, in the sheltered valley of the Rye, amidst the wild North York Moors.

Even his own abbot, the great and holy man, Aelred, described the life of the monks in austere terms:

> 'Our food is scanty, our garments rough; our drink is from the stream and our sleep often upon our book. Under our tired limbs there is but a hard mat; when sleep is sweetest we must rise at a bell's bidding...there is no moment for idleness or dissipation...'

In spite of these trials, the novice knew that at Rievaulx there was a tranquillity he could find nowhere else. In these peaceful surroundings he had a sense of being near God, of fulfilling the need he had yearned to satisfy when part of the outside world,

The two aspects of life at Rievaulx, the peace and the hardship, battled in the novice's mind as he searched for the right answer. Around him there were many examples of men who had come to Rievaulx to serve God, who had forsaken the outside world for the seclusion of the monastery and had come to terms with the austere life. They had given up much, none more so than his abbot.

Aelred had been born about 1110 at Hexham in Northumbria of good Saxon stock. About 12 years later, David, the heir to the Scottish throne, visited Hexham and heard about Aelred. David had one son, Henry, whom he thought should have a companion about his own age. He requested that he be allowed to take Aelred to court so that the two boys could be brought up together. They became very close and Aelred's time at court was particularly happy. He learned quickly and his talents did not go unnoticed.

David became King of Scotland in 1124 and Aelred moved in higher circles with a quiet, unpretentious charm. His fine intellect was coupled with the ability to deal capably with practical matters and he upheld all the noble attributes of a knight.

David made him his seneschal, a position similar to that of High Steward of the Royal Household. This was a prestigious post which Aelred filled, not only with great ability and tact but also with humility for he took God into his everyday life. He served his master well for ten years until one day in 1134 he was sent by David on a mission to Archbishop Thurstan in York. On his way, and again on his way back, he stayed with Walter Espec, Lord of Helmsley, who had given land to Cistercian monks from Clairvaux to found a monastery in the Valley of the Rye in 1132.

There is no doubt that Aelred would have heard of the Cistercians and their desire to lead a more austere life than the Benedictines. He must also have known of the community which had come to Rievaulx under their abbot, William. Aelred would be curious about them and with his enquiring mind would want to know more. Accordingly, while staying with Walter Espec, he visited Rievaulx. On his return to Helmsley his mind was torn between following the life he had witnessed in this peaceful valley or returning to the good life at the court of the Scottish King.

That must have been a real tussle for there is no doubt that Aelred loved his life among his friends, but over recent years he found himself drawn more and more to the service of God. With this clash of interests he found he could not devote himself to either as fully as he wished to. By the next morning he had decided that he would return to Scotland and that, while he would continue to serve God through the work of his daily life, the desire to commit himself fully to God, in the way of the Rievaulx monks, must be banished from his mind.

The track northward from Helmsley held to the high ground above the Rye valley. The Abbey, tucked under the slopes, surrounded by trees, would not be visible from that trackway, yet, as his retinue neared it, Aelred felt its pull. It was as if the Abbey was calling him, as if it had need of him and he of it. But Aelred resisted, thinking that it was only his fanciful ideas. Suddenly, the call became irresistible and Aelred recognised that it was not the Abbey which called, but God. He turned his horse down the hillside and became a Cistercian monk that day. So Aelred knew better than most what it was like to renounce a good life for that of a monk following the strict rules of the Cistercian Order. He became Abbot in 1147 and ruled with a fatherly understanding. He was a shining example to all the members of his community, but all men are not as strong-willed nor given the same measure of determination as Aelred. In Aelred these were based on a powerful love of God, again something which he seems to have had in greater measure than most men.

Although he had this outstanding example on which to model himself, or maybe because of it, the novice, Simon, was filled with doubts about his own ability to measure up to and cope with the life of a monk at Rievaulx. Aelred knew what was going through the mind of the young novice for he could recognise from expression and action the doubt which dwelt in Simon, but he kept his counsel. He deemed it better at this stage not to interfere for he might influence the young man's decision, and that decision had to be truly an individual one, for Simon could be committing himself to God for the rest of his life.

When the novice finally came to a decision he sought permission from his abbot to leave the community. Aelred was sad that Simon had come to the conclusion that life at Rievaulx was not for him, but he made no attempt to persuade him to stay for he knew there was a greater power than his. Recalling how, in the final moment of his return to Scotland he had been drawn to Rievaulx, Aelred gave Simon permission to leave, blessed him and said, 'Ruin not thyself, brother; nevertheless thou canst not if thou wouldst.'

Simon puzzled over this remark as he left the monastery in the late afternoon. Had the Abbot thought he was ruining his life by leaving Rievaulx? But surely it would have been more ruinous to stay if he had any doubts at all about being a monk? Now doubts about his doubts began to enter his mind. Had these doubts really been strong or had he magnified them in his own mind, putting obstacles where there really were none? The novice trudged on, traversing hill and dale, moor and valley, until the sun was blazing near the western horizon, sending its golden glow flooding across the countryside. He topped a rise, and, over the tumble of trees which spilled down the hillside, he saw a building nestling in the valley below.

In the remaining sunlight its walls glowed with an ethereal sheen, striking in its evening beauty. Simon was filled with relief. He would find shelter here for the night. He was about to start down the hillside when he stopped. He stared in amazement at the building for he realised that he was looking at the abbey he had left earlier in the day.

He had walked in a circle.

The road to his destiny.

'...nevertheless thou canst not if thou wouldst.'

The words of Aelred came back to him.

His footsteps had been guided by God.

He was meant to be a monk at Rievaulx.

With a quick step and a light heart Simon hurried down the slope back to Rievaulx.

CHAPTER THIRTEEN

THE DEFIANT ABBOT

Although he was a capable man, King John (1199-1216) was selfish, vicious, cruel and tyrannical. He constantly came into conflict with the power of the Church whose influence he saw as a threat to himself. In order to try to hold back that power and also to replenish his coffers to finance his military expeditions in France, he imposed heavy taxes on the monasteries.

At this time the Abbot of the great Cistercian abbey of Fountains was also called John. He was a member of a well-to-do York family and had been abbot at Fountains' daughter house at Louth Park, Lincolnshire. He was made Abbot of Fountains in 1203 and was soon noted as a champion and benefactor of the poor.

King John imposed a tax of twelve hundred marks of silver on Fountains to be paid immediately and similar imposing taxes were made on other Cistercian houses. The Cistercian abbots led by Abbot John called for a meeting with the King which, after their unwavering insistence, he granted.

The story goes that, standing before the King and his ministers, they refused to pay the crippling taxes in full. The King's anger mounted as he stared in disbelief at the defiant abbots. These vassals, these good-for-nothing subjects, dared to oppose HIM, the King of England. His fists clenched tight and his lips set in a grim line, his gaze swathed across the rebellious abbots. There was some misgiving amongst them. They knew the power of the King and that he could be vicious against anyone who went against his rule. But they stood firm, taking heart from the power which seemed to emanate from Abbot John.

Suddenly the King's fist crashed down on the arm of his chair.

'Get these traitors from my sight!' he yelled. 'Stake them to the ground. Bring the horses from the Royal stables and trample these cursed churchmen until they are no more!'

A gasp filled the chamber. Ministers looked askance at one another. Surely the King could not impose death on these abbots. The news would shock the kingdom and could even lead to rebellion. The abbots quivered at the implication of the King's order. Terror struck at their hearts. They had come defiant to the King, expecting concessions, but instead they faced death.

The shock seemed to have frozen ministers and guards alike.

'Will no one do my bidding?' King John's voice boomed round the chamber with the thrust of demanding authority.

Glances flashed but no one seemed to want to take the lead, no one wanted to be seen to move against the authority of the Church.

The King's fist slammed his chair arm again. 'Arrest them, damn thee, arrest them!' he thundered. His tone carried the threat of dire consequences should he not be obeyed.

But before anyone could move Abbot John defiantly raised himself to his full height and, in a voice which sent a chill to the hearts of those in the chamber, called out, 'One step against these abbots is a step against the Church and brings instant excommunication!'

No one moved.

The King's eyes widened with anger and his face darkened at the defiance. He yelled to his court and his soldiers to obey their king but the imposing figure of Abbot John, bold in his attitude, dared them to fulfil the Royal demands.

Still no one moved to arrest the abbots. Though the King raged and threatened, the fear of excommunication was the stronger.

Defeated, the King sank back in his chair. He gazed surlily round the room.

'Get out of my sight. Everyone!' he snapped suddenly. 'I'll deal with all of thee in the morning and God help thee.'

The King spent a restless night, his sleep penetrated by a vivid dream in which he was brought to trial before the Cistercian abbots, found guilty and subjected to a severe scourging. He tossed and turned but could not get rid of the dream which kept recurring and such was its vividness and intensity that he could still feel the pain when he awoke. Disturbed and troubled, he consulted a priest who served at his court. The priest, interpreting the dream as a sign from God, urged the King to make peace with the abbots before even worse things happened to him.

King John called for the abbots to be brought before him. Having seen the wrath of the King the day before and knowing of his vicious, cruel streak, the abbots came with some trepidation, though they determined outwardly to show no fear. They stood before him, defiant in their gestures but knowing they could leave this room condemned men.

The King sat, erect, proud, his kingly presence emanating through the room. His eyes were cold with disdain as the abbots lined up before him. He would dearly love to show his authority. He could detect fear in all except the one who stood out before them, their leader, Abbot John. The King's eyes narrowed, there would be pleasure in bringing this man to heel. The desire to fulfil this longing was almost overwhelming, but the torture of the previous night's dream came vividly to the King.

'I trust thee has had a good night, sire?' Abbot 'John spoke quietly.

King John was startled. It was as if this man knew his thoughts. The King started. Was that a wry smile that flicked the corners of the Abbot's mouth? It almost seemed as if he knew about the dream. What devilish powers did this man have?

'I did,' replied the King, dry-mouthed. 'And thee?'

'I spent the night praying, sire. Praying for a just conclusion to our meeting.' Abbot John's eyes held the King's.

'Indeed,' replied the King haughtily. 'Then thee'll be relieved to know that I have decided to forgo the excess taxes on the monasteries. Thee all will pay only what is right.'

The abbots exchanged surprised glances which were filled with relief.

'We thank thee, sire.' Abbot John bowed to the King. 'Then thee will want us no more? We'll be away about our business.'

'Get thee gone.' The King waved his hand in dismissal.

The abbots bowed to the King. As Abbot John straightened and turned to go his eyes met the King's again and seemed to impart a message: man cannot fight the power of prayer to God.

CHAPTER FOURTEEN

'FROM FIRE AND WATER...'

The fine parish church at Bridlington on the Yorkshire coast was formerly the ten-bay nave of the church of the Augustinian Priory founded in 1137 by Walter de Gant. Dedicated to St. Mary, it became one of the wealthiest and largest monasteries belonging to the Augustinian Canons.

The priory church was used by the townspeople, even before the Dissolution of the Monasteries under Henry VIII, and the monks were held in high respect, particularly during the time of Prior John (1362-79).

John, who was born in the tiny village of Thwing, eight miles from Bridlington, was highly regarded as a holy man who set an example by his attitude to life. Under him the priory not only prospered by his wise management but it became a place of great sanctity and its influence spread far and wide. A number of miracles were attributed to John and, after his canonisation in 1401, he became known as St. John of Bridlington to distinguish him from several other saints of the same name. Such was his reputation that many pilgrims came to pray at his shrine which was in an elevated chapel behind the High Altar. It is said that he cured many sick people and that he restored the sight of a woman who had been blind for ten years.

Even after his death he seems to have answered people's entreaties. One night the whole village of Langtoft, nestling in a hollow in the Wolds, was roused by a fire which had broken out in one of the cottages occupied by an elderly widow. When the first villagers reached the scene her screams for help could be heard coming from an upstairs room. Men rushed to the door to try to make a rescue but they were driven back by the intense heat of the flames. Realising that the only means of saving the woman was by ladder, three men rushed off to get one. They lost no time in racing back with the ladder and, as they ran towards the house, they were encouraged in their efforts by the shouts of the crowd. Fixing one end of the ladder firmly in the ground they swung the other end towards the window, only to find it was too short for their purpose.

Flames roared with a greater intensity, mocking their feeble efforts. Already the thatch was alight. Smoke, ever thickening, billowed skywards. There was not a moment to lose. Some men had already rushed away to search for a longer ladder but they returned unable to find one. Alarm seized the crowd. They were helpless to rescue their neighbour who yelled her pleas for them to do something. The roof was now well alight and it would not be long before the whole structure collapsed.

A woman in the crowd fell to her knees. 'Good St. John of Bridlington,' she cried. 'I pray thee help us save our sister for we know not what to do.'

Others, seeing her, fell to their knees and offered up their prayers and petitions to the saint. Quickly the action spread through the whole crowd.

'The ladder!' someone shouted above the chanted supplications. 'The ladder!' The quiver of excitement directed everyone's attention to the ladder which had been left leaning against the wall.

Now it reached to the window! Now the widow could be rescued!

A young man jumped to his feet and raced to the ladder. He mounted it quickly, crossed over the windowsill without difficulty and a moment later, with the woman slung across his shoulder, reappeared at the window. A shout of joy went up from the crowd and then they were on their feet, their urgings boosting his confidence as he swung on to the ladder with his human load.

Eager hands helped him when he reached the bottom and the rescuers raced away from the building. They were not a moment too soon. The roof collapsed with a great roar, and showers of sparks shot skywards amidst the flames and smoke. The widow was profuse with her thanks and, when told the result of prayers to St. John of Bridlington, she led the whole community in singing praises to the saint who had saved her life.

Fisherfolk along the Yorkshire coast tell of a miraculous rescue attributed to St. John of Bridlington. In spite of the fact that their priory was set back from the shorelines, the community had an affinity with the sea and knew of its power and its fickleness.

The North Sea can be treacherous, especially with a sudden change in the weather. A voyage apparently going well can suddenly become a nightmare. So it did for five men who left the Tees in a small craft bound for London. The weather was fine when their ship left the protection of the river and met the slight swell of the sea. They crowded on more sail to take advantage of the wind and headed south. The ship answered readily and, with everything set to their liking, the men, while keeping vigilant, settled to enjoy the voyage. Water hissed along the side of the ship as its bow cleaved a way through the gentle sea. Timbers creaked and canvas cracked with a regularity which augered well for swift voyage.

South, ever south, with the coast always in sight. Redcar Scars, Hunt Cliff, Boulby Cliffs, Runswick Bay, Kettleness, Whitby. The sky was clear blue with fluffy white clouds billowing on the seaward horizon. Robin Hood's Bay, Ravenscar, Cromer Point, Scalby Ness. As they passed Scarborough, clouds were gathering but there was little to be alarmed about. Filey Brig. The wind strengthened and suddenly, as if the sea regretted its tranquillity, the waves began to heighten.

The sky darkened with an almost overpowering menace, sending a chill through the hearts of the sailors. Still they beat southwards, hoping the sea would subside as quickly as it had formed into towering waves. A blast of wind hit them, sending the ship heeling over on her beam. A huge sea flooded over her rail and swept ferociously across the deck. Men grabbed for a secure hold and gasped as the force of water beat at them, then tried to drag them overboard.

The ship shuddered like a battered fighter but she came upright and fought against the wind and sea which took an unearthly pleasure in trying to take her and her crew to a watery doom. Awesome Bempton Cliffs, towering on the starboard side, seemed to have a magnetic effect, trying to draw the ship to the jagged rocks battered by foaming waves. Though the men fought to do what they could, they felt helpless, their fate in the hands of the elements. Terror struck at their hearts.

They were past the precipitous cliffs but knew that they had to round Flamborough Head, the great chalk cliffs pointing finger-like into the North Sea. Thunder rent the air with terrifying noise, and lightning forked seawards with increasing ferocity. That solid finger of land sent the sea in all directions. Wave upon wave built up to untold heights, creating towering crests and yawning troughs. The bows of the ship dug in, then were swept up until the ship hung suspended for a frightening moment before plunging down to meet the next wave. The light had gone, shut out by the black foreboding clouds, driven by the relentless wind.

Flamborough Head, revealed in each vivid flash of lightning, was near, too near. The men threw all their energy into trying to keep the ship away from the bulk of land which could tear the heart out of their ship. Then they were past the rocky promontory but, even though that anxiety was gone, the men could not relax, for the elements seemed determined to destroy where the land had failed. Sky and sea merged in one maelstrom of a world gone mad and in the centre a tiny ship was thrown with merciless abandon. Across the heaving sea, pin pricks of light broke the darkness of the day turned night. Lightning flashes silhouetted buildings and above them the tower of a church.

'Bridlington!' the cry rang across the deck before it was tossed away by the wind.

'Can we make it?' Another shout arose, grasping at a chance of survival.

But the wind and sea howled in protest at this possibility and drove the ship further from the shore.

Hearts sank in despair. They were doomed.

'Holy John of Bridlington, help us!' The cry was rung from the heart of one of the crew when the sight of Bridlington reminded him of the stories he had heard of the holy man.

His intonation, quiet though it was, penetrated the noise all around them and reached his fellow crew men. Immediately they joined in the entreaty, praying with a deep fervour.

With an awesome tearing sound a sail split and flapped into shreds in a matter of seconds. The ship rolled in the merciless sea.

'A light! A light!' The cry directed attention to the bright light which split the darkness between the ship and Bridlington.

The crew stared in astonishment as the figure of a monk appeared silhouetted in the light. He paused for a moment, then started to walk across the waves towards the ship. As he did so the sea before him calmed to form a tranquil path, while all around the storm raged on. The men watched in awe as the figure came nearer and nearer until he was so close that the sea around the ship was still. The figure smiled at the men, laid his hand on the bow and guided the ship back to the safety of Bridlington.

CHAPTER FIFTEEN

THE FOUNDING OF KIRKSTALL ABBEY

During the 12th century, Henry de Lacy, a wealthy landowner in the valley of the Aire, seriously ill, made a vow to help the Church should he recover. That recovery took place, so he approached the Cistercian Abbot of Fountains and asked him what he should do to fulfil his vow. Seeing the opportunity to expand the monastic life, the Abbot suggested that Henry should bequest some land at Barnoldswick in Craven to enable some of his monks to start a new monastery.

Barnoldswick is first mentioned in Anglo-Saxon times when it was known as Bernulfswick. 'Wick' means 'a villa', so this was the place where Bernulf had his villa. Bernulf's settlement grew and by Norman times was of such a size that it had its own parish church. This setting may seem an odd choice by a Cistercian abbot for the Cistercians generally chose quiet and secluded places in which to build their monasteries but he may have been influenced by the fact that buildings, including a church, already existed, even though it meant sharing them with the resident parish priest and his congregation.

In May 1147, Alexander, Prior of Fountains, with 12 monks and ten lay brothers left Fountains and came to Barnoldswick to take possession of the buildings given to them. They called this new foundation the Monastery of Mount St. Mary.

The local inhabitants resented the intrusion of the newcomers and tension was fuelled by the parish priest who did not want to share his church with the monks, for he foresaw difficulties. He proved to be correct for it was not long before the times of services clashed. The monks, following the set pattern of the monastic day, did not want the secular services to interfere with their life. In their turn the priest and his flock did not want to alter service structure to accommodate newcomers and outsiders.

Clashes were inevitable and ill-feeling ran high until it got out of hand when the monks, determined to build a completely new monastery razed the church to the ground. The priest and congregation were so incensed that they took the matter to higher authority citing the monks for their outrageous action.

They had little chance of winning against the strongly established Cistercian order and against monasticism, which was seen as the rockbed of religious life and an important influence on the way of life in the countries where it thrived.

As expected the ruling went against the people of Barnoldswick:

> 'For it seemed holy and laudable that a church should fall, if so an Abbey might be built; that of the two goods the less should give place to the greater, and that the party which was most rich in fruits of devotion should prevail. And so, peace being restored, and the controversy set at rest, the brethren proceeded to promote by gentler measures the objects of their foundation.'

However, the local people still viewed the monks with antagonism and they tried to make life difficult for them. Although partly their own fault, this atmosphere was far from conducive to the peaceful religious life the monks sought. They began to think of another move and, after six years of ill-feeling, failed crops and severe winters, they left Barnoldswick. Today there is no trace of the Monastery of Mount St. Mary at Barnoldswick and its exact location is unknown. However, remarkable for a monastery which only existed six years, it is remembered in the town's Coat of Arms which bears a Cistercian symbol of three daggers.

But what of the small band of monks who set off on foot from Barnoldswick all those years ago, no doubt to the pleasure of the local people? It seems that, when travelling on business for the foundation at Barnoldswick, Abbot Alexander had come across a group of hermits living in an idyllic wooded valley through which flowed a river of fine proportions, an ideal site for the Cistercian way of life.

In conversation with one of the hermits, Seleth, he learned that this man had been living a hermit's life in the south of the country: 'One day when I awoke I heard a voice which seemed to come from the heavens. It said to me, "Arise, Seleth, and go into the province of York, and seek diligently in the valley which is called Airedale for a place known as Kirkstall, for there shault thou prepare for a brotherhood a home where they may serve my Son".

"And who is thy son?" I asked. The answer came, "I am Mary and my Son is called Jesus of Nazareth, the Saviour of the World."

I wasted no time. I knew in my heart that I had been directed to something important so I hastened north. Though I did not know this region I had no difficulty in finding this spot beside the Aire. It was as if some higher authority guided my footsteps.

I had not been here long before the men you see around me now were attracted to the type of life I was living. I thought they were the brotherhood referred to by the voice of Mary, but now thee hast found us, good Abbot, I have a feeling that you have something to do with that brotherhood, that it is not us whom Mary meant.'

'Truly, you may be right, Seleth,' replied the Abbot, 'for my community are sorely tried and I have been worried by an urge to find them a new home. This would seem an ideal place but I want no more clashes of interest. I want peace and solitude where I and my brethren can raise a church to the Glory of God and build a place where we can pursue our religious life without trouble.'

'Then we would welcome you as Mary commanded, but I have no authority to give you the land. We are here by the goodness of William de Poictou.'

Abbot Alexander studied the situation, took his leave and contacted his benefactor, Henry de Lacy. Henry listened sympathetically to the Abbot and, agreeing that a move from Barnoldswick was desirable, persuaded William de Poictou to grant land beside the River Aire to the monks in perpetuity at an annual rent of five marks.

Alexander reigned as a benign and fatherly abbot for 35 years and supervised the erection of the monastic buildings and the church, the whole being 'a monument of the skill, the taste and the perseverance of a single man'.